The Quotable
Mr. Wesley

Updated Edition

Edited by
W. Stephen Gunter, PhD

The FOUNDATION for
EVANGELISM

The Quotable Mr. Wesley, Updated Edition

The General Board of Higher Education and Ministry leads and serves The United Methodist Church in the recruitment, preparation, nurture, education, and support of Christian leaders—lay and clergy—for the work of making disciples of Jesus Christ for the transformation of the world. Its vision is that a new generation of Christian leaders will commit boldly to Jesus Christ and be characterized by intellectual excellence, moral integrity, spiritual courage, and holiness of heart and life. The General Board of Higher Education and Ministry of The United Methodist Church serves as an advocate for the intellectual life of the church. The Board's mission embodies the Wesleyan tradition of commitment to the education of laypersons and ordained persons by providing access to higher education for all persons.

Wesley's Foundery Books is named for the abandoned foundery that early followers of John Wesley transformed, which later became the cradle of London's Methodist movement.

The Quotable Mr. Wesley, Updated Edition

"

Contents

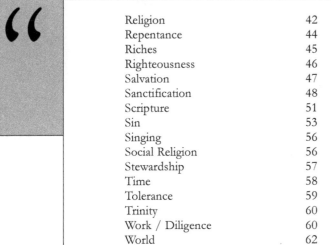

"

Preface

This updated edition of *The Quotable Mr. Wesley* by
W. Stephen Gunter, PhD, is co-sponsored by The
Foundation for Evangelism and the General Board of
Higher Education and Ministry. We hope you use it as a
catalyst to equip disciples to share the Good News of
Jesus Christ.

The Foundation for Evangelism enjoys relationship,
ministry, and partnership with a variety of Wesleyan-
tradition seminaries, churches, and organizations. It is an
independent, Wesleyan-focused foundation, devoted to
creating disciples so changed by their relationship with
Jesus Christ that they cannot stop themselves from serv-
ing as Christ served or sharing "Why Jesus" in all aspects
of their lives.

Through the generosity of its donors, and in keeping
with the doctrine, discipline, and spirit of John and
Charles Wesley, The Foundation for Evangelism endows
and invests resources so that funds will forever be used to
invite all people into a life-transforming relationship with
Jesus Christ.

The **FOUNDATION** *for*
EVANGELISM

FoundationForEvangelism.org

Abbreviations

Wesley's works are cited, whenever possible, in the bicentennial edition of *The Works of John Wesley*. If the relevant volumes have not been published yet, then older editions are used. References to *Explanatory Notes Upon the New Testament* will be given only by book, chapter, and verse since most editions are unpaginated. The following abbreviations will be used to refer to these editions:

Book of Discipline	*The Book of Discipline of The United Methodist Church.* Nashville, TN: United Methodist Publishing House, 1996.
Explanatory Notes	John Wesley, *Explanatory Notes Upon the New Testament.* London: William Bowyer, 1755.
Jackson	*The Works of the Rev. John Wesley,* edited by Thomas Jackson III, 14 vols. London: Wesleyan Methodist Book Room, 1872.
Journal	*The Journal of the Rev. John Wesley, AM,* edited by Nehemiah Curnock, 8 vols. London: Epworth Press, 1909–1916.

Letters   *The Letters of the Rev. John Wesley,*
                 edited by John Telford, 8 vols.
                 London: Epworth Press, 1931.

UMH   *United Methodist Hymnal Book*
                 of United Methodist Worship.
                 Nashville, TN: The United
                 Methodist Publishing House, 1989.

Works   *The Works of John Wesley,* begun as
                 "The Oxford Edition of the Works
                 of John Wesley" Oxford: Clarendon
                 Press, 1975–1983, continued as
                 "The Bicentennial Edition of the
                 Works of John Wesley" Nashville:
                 Abingdon Press, 1984–; 21 of 35
                 volumes published to date.

Bible/Scripture

God himself has condescended to teach the way: for this very end he came from heaven. He hath written it down in a book. O give me that book! At any price give me the Book of God! I have it. Here is knowledge enough for me. Let me be *homo unius libri.*

Works I, 105.

And the more the love of solitude is indulged the more it will increase. This is a temptation common to men. In every age and country Satan has whispered to those who began to taste the powers of the world to come (as well as to Gregory Lopez), "Au desert!" Au desert! Most of our little flock at Oxford were tried with this, my brother and I in particular. Nay, but I say, "To the Bible! To the Bible!"

Jackson, XIII, 28.

Yea, I am a Bible-bigot. I follow it in all things, both great and small.

Works XXII, 42.

Sir, if the Bible is a lie, I am as very a madman as you can conceive. But if it be true, I am in my senses. I am neither madman or enthusiast.

Works XI, 175.

I search for truth, plain Bible truth, without any regard to the praise or dispraise of men. If you will assist me in this search, more especially by showing me where I have mistaken my way, it will be gratefully acknowledged.

Jackson, XI, 449.

What are we sure of but the Bible?

Works XXII, 418.

I cannot but repeat the observation, wherein experience
confirms me more and more, that they who disbelieve the
Bible will believe anything.

Jackson, XIII, 407.

If I am an heretic, I became such by reading the Bible.
All my notions I drew from thence; and with little help
from men, unless in the single point of justification
by Faith.

Jackson, XIII, 239.

But I try every Church and every doctrine by the Bible.
This is the word by which we are to be judged in that day.

Letters, III, 172.

Now, you and I are bigots to the Bible. We think the
Bible language is like Goliath's sword: that "There is none
like it."

Letters, V, 313.

The Bible is my standard of language as well as sentiment.
I endeavour not only to think but to speak as the oracles
of God. Show me any one of the inspired writers who
mentions Christ or faith more frequently than I do, and
I will mention them more frequently.

Letters V, 8.

There are four grand and powerful arguments which
strongly induce us to believe that the Bible must be from
God, viz., miracles, prophecies, the goodness of the doctrine, and the moral character of the penman. All the miracles flow from divine power; all the prophecies, from
divine understanding; the goodness of the doctrine, from
divine goodness; and the moral character of the penmen,
from divine holiness.

Works XI, 485.

Every doctrine must stand or fall by the Bible.

Jackson X, 412.

One family, we dwell in him,
One Church, above, beneath,
Though now divided by the stream,
The narrow stream of death.

(Charles Wesley)
The United Methodist Hymnal (1989), 709.

Catholic Spirit

Every wise man therefore will allow others the same
liberty of thinking which he desires they should allow
him; and will no more insist on their embracing his opinions than he would have them to insist on his embracing
theirs. He bears with those who differ from him, and only
asks him with whom he desires to unite in love that single
question. "Is thine heart right, as my heart is with thy
heart?"

Works II, 84–85.

"Is thy heart right, as my heart is with thine?" I ask no
farther question. "If it be, give me thy hand." For opinions, or terms, let us not "destroy the work of God."
Dost thou love and serve God? It is enough. I give thee
the right hand of fellowship.

Works XIV, 42.

Communion/Lord's Supper

[I]t is the duty of every Christian to receive the Lord's
Supper as often as he can.

Works III, 428.

C

If you resolve and design to follow Christ you are fit to approach the Lord's table. If you do not design this, you are only fit for the table and company of devils.

Works III, 436.

It has been shown, first, that if we consider the Lord's Supper as a command of Christ, no man can have any pretense to Christian piety who does not receive it (not once a month, but) as often as he can; secondly, that if we consider the institution of it as a mercy to ourselves, no man who does not receive it as often as he can has any pretense to Christian prudence; thirdly, that none of the objections usually made can be any excuse for that man who does not at every opportunity obey his command and accept this mercy.

Works III, 439.

Consecration

Here is a short, a plain, an infallible rule, before you enter into particulars. In whatever profession you are engaged, you must be singular or be damned. The way to hell has nothing singular in it; but the way to heaven is singularity all over.

Works I, 672–73.

Again, the true way to heaven is a narrow way. Therefore this is another plain sure rule. "They who do not teach men to walk in a narrow way, to be singular, are false prophets."

Works I, 677.

If their eye was single, their whole body would be full of light. But suppose their eye be evil, their whole body must be full of darkness.

Works II, 527.

But so long as I can keep my eye single, and steadily fixed on the glory of God, I have no more doubt of the way wherein I should go than of the shining of the sun of noonday.

Works XXV, 398.

But let your eye be single; aim still at one thing: holy, loving faith, giving God the whole heart.

Jackson, XII, 297.

Conversion

I went to America to convert the Indians; but oh! who shall convert me?

Works XVIII, 211.

I felt my heart strangely warmed. I felt I did trust in Christ, Christ alone for salvation, and an assurance was given me that he had taken away my sins, even mine, and saved me from the law of sin and death.

Works XVIII, 250.

Evangelism

Gaining knowledge is a good thing; but saving souls is a better.

Jackson, VIII, 304.

You have nothing to do but to save souls. Therefore spend and be spent in this work. And go always, not only to those that want you, but to those that want you most.

Jackson, VIII, 310.

Indeed if thou canst save the soul of another, do; but at least save one, thy own.

Works I, 569.

Give me one hundred preachers who fear nothing but sin and desire nothing but God, and I care not a straw whether they be clergymen or laymen, such alone will shake the gates of hell and set up the kingdom of heaven upon earth.

Letters VI, 272.

Experience

Experience is sufficient to confirm a doctrine which is grounded on Scripture.

Works I, 297.

But for the proof of every one of these weighty truths experience is worth [a] thousand reasons.

Works XXV, 403.

But, although there is much advantage in long experience and we may trust an old soldier more than a novice, yet God is tied down to no rules; He frequently works a great work in a little time.

Jackson, XII, 298.

I see abundantly more than I feel. I want to feel more love and zeal for God.

Jackson, XIII, 66.

Faith

A string of opinions is no more Christian faith, than a string of beads is Christian holiness.

Jackson, X, 73.

Exhort him to press on by all possible means till he passes "from faith to faith," from the faith of a servant to the faith of a son: from the spirit of bondage unto fear, to the spirit of childlike love. He will then have "Christ revealed in his heart," enabling him to testify, "The life that I now live in the flesh I live by faith in the Son of God, who loved me, and gave himself for me"—the proper voice of a child of God.

Works IV, 35–36.

Faith is that divine evidence whereby the spiritual man discerneth God and the things of God. It is with regard to the spiritual world what sense is with regard to the natural. It is the spiritual sensation of every soul that is born of God.

Works XI, 46.

The imagination that faith supersedes holiness is the marrow of antinomianism.

Works IV, 148.

Justifying faith implies, not only a divine evidence or conviction that "God was in Christ, reconciling the world unto himself," but a sure trust and confidence that Christ died for my sins, that He loved me and gave Himself for me.

Works I, 194.

Exactly as we are justified by faith, so are we sanctified by faith. Faith is the condition, and the only condition of sanctification, exactly as it is of justification. It is the condition: none is sanctified but he that believes; without faith no man is sanctified.

Works II, 163.

Christian faith is then not only an assent to the whole Gospel of Christ, but also a full reliance on the blood of Christ, a trust in the merits of his life, death, and resurrection; a recumbency on him as our atonement and our life, as given for us, and living in us.

Works I, 121.

There is no true faith, that is, justifying faith, which hath not the righteousness of Christ for its object.

Works I, 454.

His pardoning mercy supposes nothing in us but a sense of mere sin and misery; and to all who see, and feel, and own their wants, and their utter inability to remove them, God freely gives faith, for the sake of him "in whom he is always well pleased."

Works XI, 48–49.

Free Will

Natural free-will, in the present state of mankind, I do not understand: I only assert, that there is a measure of free-will supernaturally restored to every man, together with that supernatural light which "enlightens every man that cometh into the world."

Jackson, X, 229–30.

Freethinkers

Freethinkers, so called, are seldom close thinkers.

Works, XXII, 134.

Grace

To retain the grace of God is much more than to gain it:
Hardly one in three does this.

Jackson, XIII, 104.

The best of all is, God is with us.

Jackson, V, 547.

To use the grace we have, and now to expect all we want,
is the grand secret.

Letters IV, 313–14.

[I]t is a sad observation that they that have most money
have usually least grace.

Jackson, XIII, 70.

Grace is the source, faith the condition, of salvation.

Works I, 118.

I am more and more inclined to think that there are
none living so established in grace but that they may
possibly fall.

Jackson, XII, 357.

First, it (grace) is free in all to whom it is given. It does
not depend on any power or merit in man; no, not in any
degree, neither in whole nor in part. It does not in any

wise depend either on the good works or righteousness
of the receiver; not on anything he has done, or anything
he is.

Works III, 545.

Look up, and receive a fresh supply of Grace!

Letters, VI, 21.

How admirably pardon and holiness are comprised in that
one word, "grace!"

Jackson, XII, 429.

We need great grace to converse with great people!

Works XXI, 142.

The grace or love of God, whence cometh our salvation,
is free in all, and free for all.

Works III, 544.

The sympathies formed by grace far surpass those formed
by nature.

Jackson, XI, 435.

Heartfelt Religion

"Is thy heart right, as my heart is with thine?" I ask no
farther question. "If it be, give me thy hand." For opinions, or terms, let us not "destroy the work of God."
Dost thou love and serve God? It is enough. I give thee
the right hand of fellowship.

Works IX, 42.

But our comfort is, He that made the heart can heal
the heart.

Jackson, XIII, 125.

Give Him your will, and you give Him your heart.
Jackson, XII, 294.

Whatever is spoke of the religion of the heart, and of the inward workings of the Spirit of God, must appear enthusiasm to those who have not felt them; that is, if they take upon them to judge of the things which they own they know not.

Works XIX, 121–22.

Unite the two so long disjoined,
    Knowledge and vital piety:
Learning and holiness combined.
        (Composed by Charles Wesley for the opening of
        the Kingswood School for Children, June 24, 1748.)
        Works VII, 644.

Heaven

I want to know one thing, the way to heaven—how to land safe on that happy shore. God himself has condescended to teach the way: for this very end he came from heaven. He hath written it down in a book. O give me that book!

Works I, 105.

Whosoever will reign with Christ in heaven, must have Christ reigning in him on earth.

Jackson X, 364.

Holiness

Go on, in a full pursuit of all the mind that was in Christ, of inward and then outward holiness; so shall you be not almost but altogether a Christian.

Works III, 332.

It (Christianity) is holiness and happiness, the image of God impressed on a created spirit, a fountain of peace and love springing up into everlasting life.

Jackson X, 75.

As the more holy we are upon earth the more happy we must be (seeing there is an inseparable connection between holiness and happiness).

Works II, 431.

But we must love God before we can be holy at all; this being the root of all holiness.

Works I, 274.

Always, remember the essence of Christian holiness is simplicity and purity; one design, one desire entire devotion to God. But this admits of a thousand degrees and variations, and certainly it will be proved by a thousand temptations; but in all these things you shall be more than conqueror.

Jackson XII, 289.

There is no such height or strength of holiness as it is impossible to fall from.

Jackson XI, 426.

Christian perfection therefore does not imply (as some men seem to have imagined) an exemption either from ignorance or mistake, or infirmities or temptations. Indeed, it is only another term for holiness.

Works II, 104.

A thousand infirmities are consistent even with the highest degree of holiness, which is no other than pure love, an heart devoted to God, one design and one desire.

Jackson XII, 386.

By holiness I mean, not fasting, or bodily austerity, or any other external means of improvement, but that inward temper to which all these are subservient, a renewal of soul in the image of God.

Works XXV, 399.

For as there is but one heaven, so there is but one way to it even the way of faith in Christ (for we speak not of opinions, or outward modes of worship), the way of love to God and man, the "highway of holiness."

Works XI, 291.

And what is Christian liberty but another word for holiness? And where is this liberty or holiness if it is not in the creature? Holiness is the love of God and man, or the mind which was in Christ.

Jackson, XII, 413.

The righteousness of Christ is, doubtless, necessary for any soul that enters into glory. But so is personal holiness, too, for every child of man. . . . The former is necessary to entitle us to heaven; the latter, to qualify us for it. Without the righteousness of Christ we could have no claim to glory; without holiness we could have no fitness for it.

Works IV, 144.

I have found that even the precious doctrine of Salvation by Faith has need to be guarded with the utmost care, or those who hear it will slight both inward and outward holiness.

Jackson, XII, 161.

Holy Spirit

"The inward witness, son, the inward witness," said he to me, "that is the proof, the strongest proof, of Christianity."
(Samuel Wesley, Sen.)
Works XXVI, 289.

When the witness and the fruit of the Spirit meet together, there can be no stronger proof that we are of God.

Jackson, XIII, 98.

Although no man on earth can explain the particular manner wherein the Spirit of God works on the soul, yet whosoever has these fruits cannot but know and feel that God has wrought them in his heart.

Jackson, XIII, 49.

But perhaps one might say (desiring any who are taught of God to correct, to soften or strengthen the expression), the testimony of the Spirit is an inward impression on the soul, whereby the Spirit of God directly "witnesses to my spirit that I am a child of God;" that Jesus Christ hath loved me, and given himself for me; that all my sins are blotted out, and I, even I, am reconciled to God.

Works I, 274.

Justification

This then is the salvation which is through faith, even in the present world; a salvation from sin and the consequences of sin, both often expressed in the word "justification," which, taken in the largest sense, implies a deliverance from guilt and punishment, by the atonement of Christ actually applied to the soul of the sinner now believing on him, and a deliverance from the power of sin, through Christ "formed in his heart." So that he who is thus justified or saved by faith is indeed "born again."

Works I, 124.

[I]t [justification] is not the being made actually just and righteous. This is sanctification; which is indeed in some degree the immediate fruit of justification, but nevertheless is a distinct gift of, God, and of a totally different nature. The one implies what God does for us through his Son; the other what he works in us by his Spirit.

Works I, 187.

[The clergy who dissent from the Church of England] speak of justification, either as the same thing with sanctification, or as something consequent upon it. I believe justification to be wholly distinct from sanctification, and necessarily antecedent to it.

Works, XIX, 96.

I believe three things must go together in our justification: upon God's part, his great mercy and grace; upon Christ's part, the satisfaction of God's justice, by the offering his body and shedding his blood, "and fulfilling the law of God perfectly," and upon our part, true and living faith in the merits of Jesus Christ.

Works IX, 51.

Justification is another word for pardon. It is the forgiveness of all our sins, and (what is necessarily implied therein) our acceptance with God. The price whereby this hath been procured for us (commonly termed the "meritorious cause" of our justification) is the blood and righteousness of Christ, or (to express it a little more clearly) all that Christ hath done and suffered for us till "he poured out his soul for the transgressors."

Works II, 157–58.

From the moment we are justified, there may be a gradual sanctification, a growing in grace, a daily advance in the knowledge and love of God.

Jackson, VIII, 329.

The plain scriptural notion of justification is pardon, the forgiveness of sins. It is that act of God the Father whereby, for the sake of the propitiation made by the blood of his Son, he "showeth forth his righteousness (or mercy) by the sins that are past."

Works I, 189.

I believe no good works can be previous to justification; nor, consequently, a condition of it.

Jackson, I, 225.

God justifieth not the godly, but the ungodly; not those that are holy already, but the unholy.

Works I, 191.

I think on Justification just as I have done any time these seven-and-twenty years, and just as Mr. Calvin does. In this respect I do not differ from him an hair's breadth.

Jackson, III, 212.

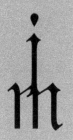

But though it be allowed that justification and the new birth are in point of time inseparable from each other, yet are they easily distinguished as being not the same, but things of a widely different nature. Justification implies only a relative, the new birth a real change.

Works I, 431.

Means of Grace

By "means of grace" I understand outward signs, words, or actions ordained of God, and appointed for this end to be the ordinary channels whereby he might convey to men preventing, justifying, or sanctifying grace. . . . The chief of these means are prayer, whether in secret or with the great congregation; searching the scripture (which implies reading, hearing, and meditating thereon) and receiving the Lord's Supper, eating bread and drinking wine in remembrance of him; and these we believe to be ordained of God as the ordinary channels of conveying his grace to the souls of men.

Works I, 381.

I contend that all the ordinances of God are the stated channels of his grace to man; and that it is our bounden duty to use them all, at all possible opportunities.

Works XI, 418.

Methodist Identity

Our main doctrines, which include all the rest, are three, that of repentance, of faith, and of holiness. The first of these we account, as it were, the porch of religion; the next, the door, the third, religion itself.

Works. IX, 227.

God's design was . . . not to form any new sect; but to reform the nation, particularly the Church; and to spread Scriptural holiness over the land.

Jackson, VIII, 299–300.

From this short sketch of Methodism, (so called,) any man of understanding may easily discern that it is only plain, scriptural religion, guarded by a few prudential regulations. The essence of it is holiness of heart and life; the circumstantials all point to this.

Works IX, 529.

But as to all opinions which do not strike at the root of Christianity, we think and let think.

Works IX, 34.

Nothing can be more simple, nothing more rational, than the Methodist discipline; it is entirely founded on common sense, particularly applying the general rules of Scripture. Any person determined to save his soul may be united (this is the only condition required) with them. But this desire must be evidenced by three marks: avoiding all known sin, doing good after his power, and attending all the ordinances of God.

Works III, 511.

Methodism, so called, is the old religion, the religion of the Bible, the religion of the primitive Church, the religion of the Church of England.

Works III, 585.

[A] Methodist is one who has "the love of God shed abroad in his heart by the Holy Ghost given unto him;" one who "loves the Lord his God with all his heart, and with all his soul, and with all his mind, and with all his strength." God is the joy of his heart, and the desire of his soul.

Works IX, 35.

This doctrine (entire sanctification) is the grand depositum which God has lodged with the people called Methodists; and for the sake of propagating this chiefly He appears to have raised us up.

Jackson, XIII, 9.

It is the glory of the people called Methodists that they condemn none for their opinions or modes of worship. They think and let think, and insist upon nothing but faith working by love.

Letters, VII, 190.

Better forty members should be lost than our discipline lost. They are no Methodists that will bear no restraints.

Jackson, XIII, 164.

Be exact in every point of discipline. Keep your rules, and they will keep you.

Letters, VIII, 22.

The fundamental doctrine of the people called Methodists is, Whosoever will be saved, before all things it is necessary that he hold the true faith; the faith which works by love; which, by means of the love of God and our neighbour, produces both inward and outward holiness.

Jackson, III, 24.

We look upon ourselves, not as the authors or ringleaders of a particular sect or party; (it is the farthest thing from our thoughts;) but as messengers of God to those who are Christians in name, but Heathens in heart and in life, to call them back to that from which they are fallen, to real genuine Christianity.

Works IX, 337.

Unity and holiness are the two things I want among the Methodists. Who will rise up with me against all open or secret opposers either of one or the other?

Letters, V, 4.

I am not afraid that the people called Methodists should ever cease to exist either in Europe or America. But I am afraid, lest they should only exist only as a dead sect, having the form of religion without the power. And this undoubtedly will be the case, unless they hold fast both the doctrine, spirit, and discipline with which they first set out.

Works IX, 527.

By Methodists I mean a people who profess to pursue (in whatsoever measure they have attained) holiness of heart and life, inward and outward conformity in all things to the revealed will of God; who place religion in an uniform resemblance of the great object of it; in a steady imitation of Him they worship in all his imitable perfections; more particularly injustice, mercy, and truth, or universal love filling the heart, and governing the life.

Works IX, 123–24.

And the Methodist knave is the worst of all knaves.

Jackson, VIII, 302.

Unite the two so long disjoined,
    Knowledge and vital piety:
Learning and holiness combined.

Works VII, 644.

The Methodists must take heed to their DOCTRINE, their EXPERIENCE, their PRACTICE, and their DISCIPLINE. If they attend to their doctrines only, they will make the people antinomians; if to the experimental part of religion only, they will make them Pharisees; and if they do not attend to their discipline, they will be like persons who bestow much pain in cultivating their garden, and put no fence round it, to save it from the wild boar of the forest.

Wesleyan Methodist Magazine 48 (1825), 390.

My design was not only to direct them how to press after perfection, to exercise their every grace and improve every talent they had received, and to incite them to love one another more, and to watch more carefully over each other, but also to have a select company to whom I might unbosom myself on all occasions without reserve.

Jackson, VIII, 260.

The Methodists alone do not insist on your holding this or that opinion; but they think and let think. Neither do they impose any particular mode of worship; but you may continue to worship in your former manner, be it what it may.

Jackson, IV, 419.

New Birth

If any doctrines within the whole compass of Christianity may be properly termed fundamental they are doubtless these two: the doctrine of justification, and that of the new birth; the former relating to that great work which God does for us, in forgiving our sins; the latter to the great work which God does in us, in renewing our fallen nature.

Works II, 187.

n

When we are born again, then our sanctification, our inward and outward holiness begins. And thenceforward we are gradually to "grow up in him who is our head."
Works II, 198.

I believe it [the new birth] to be an inward thing; a change from inward wickedness to inward goodness; an entire change of our inmost nature from the image of the devil (wherein we are born) to the image of God; a change from the love of the creature to the love of the Creator; from earthly and sensual to heavenly and holy affections in a word, a change from the tempers of the spirit of darkness to those of the angels of God in heaven.
Works XIX, 97.

But though it be allowed that justification and the new birth are in point of time inseparable from each other, yet are they easily distinguished as being not the same, but things of a widely different nature. Justification implies only a relative, the new birth a real, change.
Works I, 431.

It [the new birth] is that great change which God works in the soul when he brings it into life; when he raises it from the death of sin to the life of righteousness. It is the change wrought in the whole soul by the almighty Spirit of God when it is "created anew in Christ Jesus."
Works II, 193–94.

[B]aptism is not the new birth. . . . But indeed the reason of the thing is so clear and evident as not to need any other authority. For what can be more plain than that the one is an external, the other an internal work? That the one is a visible, the other an invisible thing, and therefore wholly different from each other: the one being an act of man, purifying the body, the other a change wrought by

God in the soul. So that the former is just as distinguishable from the latter as the soul from the body, or water from the Holy Ghost.

Works II, 197.

Orthodoxy

A man may be orthodox in every point, he may not only espouse right opinions, but zealously defend them against all opposers; he may think justly concerning the incarnations of our Lord, concerning the ever blessed Trinity, and every other doctrine contained in the oracles of God. He may assent to all the three creeds that called the Apostles', the Nicene, and the Athanasian and yet 'tis possible he may have no religion at all, no more than a Jew, Turk or pagan. He may be almost as orthodox as the devil (though indeed not altogether; for every man errs in something, whereas we can't well conceive him [the devil] to hold any erroneous opinion) and may all the while be as great a stranger as he to the religion of the heart.

Works I, 220–21.

Orthodoxy, I say, or right opinion, is at best but a very slender part of religion, if any part of it at all.

Works X, 347.

Perfection

By "perfection" I mean "perfect love," or the loving God with all our heart, so as to rejoice evermore, to pray without ceasing and everything to give thanks. I am convinced every believer may attain this; yet I do not say he is in a state of damnation or under the curse of God till he does attain. No, he is in a state of grace and in favour with God as long as he believes.

Works II, 227.

To set the state of perfection too high is the surest way to drive it out of the world.

Works XII, 445.

What is Christian perfection? The loving God with all our heart, mind, soul, and strength. This implies that no wrong temper, non contrary to love, remains in the soul; and that all the thoughts, words, and actions are governed by pure love.

Works XI, 394.

It [perfection] is amissible, capable of being lost.

Jackson XI, 442.

Thus much is certain: they that love God with all their heart and all men as themselves are scripturally perfect. And surely such there are; otherwise the promise of God would be a mere mockery of human weakness. Hold fast this. But then remember, on the other hand, you have this treasure in an earthen vessel; you dwell in a poor, shattered house of clay, which presses down the immortal spirit. Hence all your thoughts, words, and actions are so imperfect, so far from coming up to the standard (that law of love which, but for the corruptible body, your soul would answer in all instances) that you may well say it till you go to Him you love: Every moment, Lord, I need the merit of Thy death.

Works XII, 279.

It is certain every babe in Christ has received the Holy Ghost, and the Spirit witnesses with his spirit that he is a child of God. But he has not obtained Christian perfection. Perhaps you have not considered St. John's threefold distinction of Christian believers; little children, young men, and fathers. All of the these had received the Holy Ghost; but only the fathers were perfected in love.

Letters, VI, 146.

By perfection I mean the humble, gentle, patient love of God and man, ruling all the tempers, words, and actions; the whole heart, and the whole life.

Letters, IV, 187.

Christian perfection therefore does not imply (as some men seem to have imagined) an exemption either from ignorance or mistake, or infirmities or temptations. Indeed, it is only another term for holiness.

Works VIII, 257.

I should wonder if the scarecrow of sinless perfection was not brought in some way or other.

Works VIII, 432.

As to the word [perfection], it is scriptural; therefore neither you nor I can in conscience object against it, unless we would send the Holy Ghost to school and teach Him to speak who made the tongue.

Works XII, 257.

"Absolute and infallible perfection?" I never contended for it. Sinless perfection? Neither do I contend for this, seeing the term is not scriptural. A perfection that perfectly fulfills the whole law, and so needs not the merits of Christ? I acknowledge none such I do now, and always did, protest against it.

Works XII, 257.

There are two general ways wherein it pleases God to lead
His children to perfection—doing and suffering. And let
Him take one or the other, we are assured. His way is
best.

Letters VI, 75.

It is not possible to avoid all pleasure, even of sense,
without destroying the body.

Jackson XI, 461.

Neither can any man while he is in a corruptible body
attain to Adamic perfection.

Works XI, 412.

No one then is so perfect in this life as to be free from
ignorance. Nor, secondly, from mistake, which indeed is
almost an unavoidable consequence of it; seeing those
who "know but in part" are ever liable to err touching the
things which they know not.

Works II, 101–2.

It [perfection] is nothing higher and nothing lower than
this, the pure love of God and man; the loving God with
all our heart and soul, and our neighbour as ourselves. It
is love governing the heart and life, running through all
our tempers, words, and actions.

Jackson XI, 397.

One word more, concerning setting perfection too high.
That perfection which I believe, I can boldly preach,
because I think I see five hundred witnesses of it. Of that
perfection which you preach, you do not even think you
see any witness at all. . . . I still think to set perfection so
high is effectually to renounce it.

Jackson XII, 131.

Plain Truth

I design plain truth for plain people. Therefore of set purpose I abstain from all nice and philosophical speculations, from all perplexed and intricate reasonings, and as far as possible from even the show of learning, unless in sometimes citing the original Scriptures. I labour to avoid all words which are not easy to be understood, all which are not used in common life. . . . Yet I am not assured that I do not sometimes slide into them unawares; it is so extremely natural to imagine that a word which is familiar to ourselves is so to all the world.

Works I, 104.

I desire your words may be always the picture of your heart. This is truly "plain language."

Works XI, 255.

I thoroughly agree that it is best to "use the most common words and that in the most obvious sense," and have been diligently labouring after this very thing for little less than twenty years. I am not conscious of using any uncommon word, or any words which are the constant language of Holy Writ. These I purposely use, desiring always to express Scripture sense in Scripture phrase.

Works XXVI, 155.

Nothing here appears in an elaborate, elegant, or oratorical dress. If it had been my desire or design to write thus, my leisure would not permit. But in truth I at present designed nothing less, for I now write (as I generally speak) *ad populum* to the art of speaking, but who notwithstanding are competent judges of those truths which are necessary to present and future happiness.

Works I, 103–4.

P o o r / P o v e r t y

So wickedly, devilishly false is that common objection,
"They are poor only because they are idle."

Works XX, 445.

I love the poor, in many of them I find pure genuine
grace, unmixed with paint, folly, and affectation.

Works XII, 200.

The poor are the Christians. I am quite out of conceit
with almost all those who have this world's goods.

Works XIII, 71.

If you cannot relieve, do not grieve, the poor. Give them
soft words, if nothing else.

Works XX, 176.

I visited as many as I could of the sick. How much better
is it, when it can be done, to carry relief to the poor, than
to send it! and that for our own sake and theirs. For
theirs, as it is so much more comfortable to them, and as
we may then assist them in spirituals as well as temporals;
and for our own, as it is far more apt to soften our heart,
and to make us naturally care for each other.

Works XXI, 290.

I bear the rich, and love the poor.

Letters, IV, 266.

One great reason why the rich have so little sympathy for
the poor is because they so seldom visit them.

Works III, 387.

I have found some of the uneducated poor who have
exquisite taste and sentiment; and many, very many,

of the rich who have scarcely any at all. . . . And they have (many of them) faith and the love of God in a larger measure than any person I know.

Works XII, 301.

Prayer

Prayer may be said to be the breath of our spiritual life.

Explanatory Notes: I Thess. 5:16.

And indeed our prayers are the proper test of our desires, nothing being fit to have a place in our desires which is not fit to have a place in our prayers.

Works I, 578.

I was surprised to hear an extemporary prayer and a written sermon. Are not then the words we speak to God to be set in order at least as carefully as those we speak to our fellow-worms!

Works XVIII, 460.

Prayer continues in the desire of the heart, though the understanding be employed on outward things.

Jackson XI, 438.

Above all, add to the rest (for it is not labour lost) that old unfashionable medicine, prayer.

Jackson XIV, 327.

Nature and the devil will always oppose private prayer; but it is worth while to break through. That it is a cross will not hinder its being a blessing: Nay, often the more reluctance, the greater blessing.

Jackson XII, 201.

Watch, that ye may pray; and pray, that ye may watch.
Explanatory Notes: I Pet. 4:7.

You may as well expect a child to grow without food as a soul without private prayer.

Letters, IV, 272.

I always use a short private prayer when I attend the public service of God. Do not you? Why do you not? Is not this according to the Bible?

Works XXII, 169.

I always kneel before the Lord my Maker, when I pray in public.

Works XXII, 43.

For many years I had a kind of scruple with regard to praying for temporal things. But three or four years ago I was thoroughly persuaded that scruple was unnecessary. Being then straitened much, I made it a matter of prayer, and I had an immediate answer. It is true we can only ask outward blessings with reserve. "If this is best; if it be thy will." And in this manner we may certainly plead the promise, "All these things shall be added unto you."

Jackson XII, 376.

By our reading prayers we prevent our people's contracting an hatred for forms of prayer, which would naturally be the case if we always prayed extempore.

Jackson XIII, 113.

[O]ne great office of prayer is . . . to exercise our dependence on God; to increase our desire of the things we ask for, to make us so sensible of our wants, that we may never cease wrestling till we have prevailed for the blessing.

Explanatory Notes: Matt. 6:8.

God does nothing but in answer to prayer: and even they who have been converted to God, without praying for it themselves (which is exceeding rare,) were not without the prayers of others. Every new victory which a soul gains is the effect of a new prayer.

Jackson XI, 437.

Believing one reason of my want of joy was want of time for prayer, I resolved to do no business till I went to church in the morning, but to continue pouring out my heart before him. And this day my spirit was enlarged; so that though I was now also assaulted by many temptations, I was more than conqueror, gaining more power thereby to trust and to rejoice in God my Saviour.

Works XVIII, 251–52.

Preaching

Give me one hundred preachers who fear nothing but sin and desire nothing but God, and I care not a straw whether they be clergymen or laymen, such alone will shake the gates of hell and set up the Kingdom of God upon earth.

Letters, VI, 272.

If we could once bring all our preachers, itinerant and local, uniformly and steadily to insist on those two points, "Christ dying for us" and "Christ reigning in us," we should shake the trembling gates of hell.

Jackson XII, 460.

At four in the afternoon, I submitted to be more vile, and proclaimed in the highways the glad tidings of salvation, speaking from a little eminence in a ground adjoining to the city, to about three thousand people.

Works XIX, 46.

What marvel the devil does not love field-preaching!
Neither do I: I love a commodious room, a soft cushion, a
handsome pulpit. But where is my zeal, if I do not trample
all these underfoot in order to save one more soul?

Works XXI, 203.

Not that I would advise to preach the law without the
gospel, any more than the gospel without the law.
Undoubtedly both should be preached in their turns; yea,
both at once, or both in one. All the conditional promises
are instances of this: they are law and gospel mixed
together.

Works XXVI, 485.

I know, were I myself to preach one whole year in one
place, I should preach both myself and most of my congregation asleep. Nor can I ever believe it was ever the
will of our Lord that any congregation should have one
teacher only. We have found by long and constant experience that a frequent change of teachers is best.

Jackson VIII, 199.

Field-preaching was therefore a sudden expedient, a thing
submitted to rather than chosen, and therefore submitted
to because I thought preaching even thus better than not
preaching at all.

Works XI, 178.

I allow that it is highly expedient whoever preaches in his
name should have an outward as well as an inward call;
but that it is absolutely necessary I deny.

Works II, 74.

I often speak loud, often vehemently; but I never scream,
I never strain myself. I dare not; I know it would be a sin
against God and my own soul.

Jackson XII, 331.

I wonder at those who still talk so loud of the indecency of field-preaching. The highest indecency is in St. Paul's Church, when a considerable part of the congregation are asleep, or talking, or looking about, not minding a word the preacher says.

Works XX, 245.

Preaching the Gospel

I mean by "preaching the gospel" preaching the love of God to sinners, preaching the life, death, resurrection, and intercession of Christ, with all the blessings which in consequence thereof are freely given to true believers.

Works XXVI, 482.

If I might choose, I should still (as I have done hitherto) preach the gospel to the poor.

Works XXI, 233.

If we could once bring all our preachers, itinerant and local, uniformly and steadily to insist on those two points, "Christ dying for us" and "Christ reigning in us," we should shake the trembling gates of hell.

Jackson XII, 460.

If a believer make shipwreck of the faith, he is no longer a child of God. And then he may go to hell, yea, and certainly will, if he continues in unbelief.

Jackson X, 297.

Reason

Passion and prejudice govern the world, only under the name of reason. It is our part, by religion and reason joined, to counteract them all we can.

Jackson XII, 412–13.

I am very rarely led by impressions, but generally by reason and by Scripture.

Jackson XIII, 66.

It is a fundamental principle with us that to renounce reason is to renounce religion, that religion and reason go hand in hand, and that all irrational religion is false religion.

Works IX, 382.

When persons are governed by passion rather than reason, we can expect little good.

Letters, V, 217.

By reason we learn what is that new birth, without which we cannot enter into the kingdom of heaven, and what that holiness is, without which no man shall see the Lord.

Works II, 592.

[I]t [reason] is utterly incapable of giving either faith, or hope or love; and consequently of producing either real virtue or substantial happiness.

Works II, 600.

True Religion is the highest reason. It is indeed wisdom, virtue, and happiness in one.

Letters, IV, 118.

Religion

O what is so scarce as learning, save religion!

Works VII, 459.

Ye know that the great end of religion is to renew our hearts in the image of God, to repair that total loss of righteousness and true holiness which we sustained by the sin of our first parent.

Works II, 185.

I entirely agree with you that religion is love and peace and joy in the Holy Ghost; that as it is the happiest, so it is the cheerfullest thing in the world; that [it] is inconsistent with moroseness, sourness, severity, and indeed with whatever is not according to the softness, sweetness, and gentleness of Jesus Christ.

Works XXV, 500.

But to refine religion is to spoil it. It is the most simple thing that can be conceived: it is only humble, gentle, patient love.

Jackson XIII, 165–66.

I have one point in view to promote, so far as I am able: vital, practical religion; and by the grace of God to beget, preserve, and increase the life of God in the souls of men.

Jackson XIII, 197.

By religion I mean the love of God and man, filling the heart and governing the life. The sure effect of this is the uniform practice of justice, mercy, and truth.

Works III, 448.

r

[R]eligion has nothing sour, austere, unsociable, unfriendly in it, but on the contrary implies the most winning sweetness, the most amiable softness and gentleness.

Works XXV, 502.

"What is religion, then?" It is easy to answer if we consult the oracles of God. According to these it lies in one single point: it is neither more or less than love; it is love which "is the fulfilling of the law," "the end of the commandment." Religion is the love of God and our neighbour that is, every man under heaven.

Works III, 189.

True religion is right tempers towards God and man. It is in two words, gratitude and benevolence: gratitude to our Creator and supreme Benefactor, and benevolence to our fellow-creatures. In other words, it is the loving God with all our heart, and our neighbour as ourselves.

Works IV, 66–67.

In religion, I am for as few innovations as possible. I love the old wine best.

Jackson XII, 438.

Do we not many times dispense with religion and reason together because we would not "look particular?" Are we not often more afraid of being out of the fashion than of being out of the way of salvation?

Works I, 565.

"What then is religion?" It is happiness in God, or in the knowledge and love of God. It is "faith working by love," producing "righteousness and peace and joy in the Holy Ghost."

Jackson XIII, 132.

"Holy solitaries" is a phrase no more consistent with the gospel than holy adulterers. The gospel of Christ knows of no religion, but social; no holiness but social holiness.

Jackson XIV, 321.

Repentance

Repentance frequently means an inward change, a change of mind from sin to holiness. But we now speak of it in a quite difference sense, as it is one kind of self-knowledge the knowing ourselves sinners, yea, guilty, helpless sinners, even though we know we are children of God.

Works I, 336.

It is allowed also that repentance "and fruits meet for repentance" go before faith. Repentance absolutely must go before faith; fruits "meet for it" if there be opportunity. By repentance I mean conviction of sin producing real desires and sincere resolutions of amendment; and by "fruits meet for repentance" forgiving our brother, ceasing from evil, doing good, using the ordinances of God, and in general obeying him according to the measure of grace, which we have received.

Works XI, 106.

The terms of acceptance for fallen man are, repentance and faith. "Repent ye, and believe the gospel."

Jackson X, 322.

[R]epentance and its fruits are only remotely necessary, necessary in order to faith; whereas faith is immediately and directly necessary to justification. It remains that faith is the only condition which is immediately and proximately necessary to justification.

Works II, 163.

Riches

For wherever true Christianity spreads it must cause diligence and frugality, which, is the natural course of things, must beget riches. And riches naturally beget pride, love of the world, and every temper that is destructive of Christianity.

Works IV 95–96.

Riches are equally a hindrance to the loving our neighbour as ourselves, that is, to the loving all mankind as Christ loved us.

Works III, 522.

How, then, is it possible that Methodism, that is, the religion of the heart, though it flourishes now as a green bay tree, should continue in this state? For the Methodists in every place grow diligent and frugal; consequently, they increase in goods. Hence they proportionably increase in pride, in anger, in the desire of the flesh, the desire of the eyes, and the pride of life. So although the form of religion remains, the spirit is swiftly vanishing away.

Works IX, 530.

You know that in seeking happiness from riches you are only striving to drink out of empty cups. And let them be painted and gilded ever so finely, they are empty still.

Works III, 240–41.

But still remember: riches have in all ages been the bane of genuine Christianity.

Works II, 468.

We are not at liberty to use what he has lodged in our hands as we please, but as he pleases, who alone is the possessor of heaven and earth, and the Lord of every creature. We have no right to dispose of anything we have but according to his will, seeing we are not proprietors of any of these things.

Works II, 283–84.

[Gold and silver is] an excellent gift of God, answering the noblest ends. In the hands of his children it is food for the hungry, drink for the thirsty, raiment for the naked. It gives to the traveller and the stranger where to lay his head. By it we may supply the place of an husband to the widow, and of a father to the fatherless.

Works II, 268.

[R]iches and happiness seldom dwell together.

Works III, 345.

If poverty contracts and depresses the mind, riches sap its fortitude, destroy its vigour, and nourish its caprices.

Letters, V, 180.

Righteousness

The righteousness of Christ is, doubtless, necessary for any soul that enters into glory. But so is personal holiness, too, for every child of man. . . . The former is necessary to entitle us to heaven; the latter, to qualify us for it. Without the righteousness of Christ we could have no claim to glory; without holiness we could have no fitness for it.

Works IV, 144.

The first thing then which admits of no dispute among reasonable men is this: to all believers the righteousness of Christ is imputed; to unbelievers it is not.

Works I, 454.

But a man may be righteous before he does what is right; holy in heart before he is holy in life.

Jackson IX, 292.

Righteousness is, properly and directly, a right temper or disposition of mind, or a complex of all right tempers.

Jackson IX, 342.

For the kingdom of God—That is, true religion, does not consist in external observances. But in righteousness— The image of God stamped on the heart; the love of God and man, accompanied with the peace that passeth all understanding, and joy in the Holy Ghost.

Explanatory Notes: Rom. 14:17.

Salvation

By salvation I mean . . . a present deliverance from sin, a restoration of the soul to its primitive health, its original purity; a recovery of the divine nature.

Works XI, 106.

Salvation is carried on by "convincing grace," usually in scripture termed "repentance," which brings a larger measure of self-knowledge, and a farther deliverance from the heart of stone. Afterwards we experience the proper Christian salvation; whereby, "through grace" we "are saved by faith," consisting of those two grand branches, justification and sanctification. By justification we are saved from the guilt of sin, and restored to the favour of God; by sanctification we are saved from the power and root of sin, and restored to the image of God.

Works III, 204.

I have found that even the precious doctrine of Salvation by Faith has need to be guarded with the utmost care, or those who hear it will slight both inward and outward holiness.

Jackson XII, 161.

This then is the salvation which is through faith, even in the present world: a salvation from sin and the consequences of sin, both often expressed in the word "justification," which, taken in the largest sense, implies a deliverance from guilt and punishment, by the statement of Christ actually applied to the soul of the sinner now believing on him, and a deliverance from the power of sin, through Christ "formed in his heart." So that he who is thus justified, or saved by faith, is indeed "born again."

Works I, 124.

It [salvation] is not something at a distance: it is a present thing, a blessing which, through the free mercy of God, ye are now in possession of. Nay, the words may be rendered, and that with equal propriety, "Ye have been saved." So that the salvation which is here spoken of might be extended to the entire work of God, from the first dawning of grace in the soul till it is consummated in glory.

Works II, 156.

Sanctification

[I]t [justification] is not the being made actually just and righteous. This is sanctification; which is indeed in some degree the immediate fruit of justification, but nevertheless is a distinct gift of God, and of a totally different nature. The one implies what God does for us through his Son; the other what he works in us by his Spirit.

Works I, 187.

[The clergy who dissent from the Church of England] speak of justification, either as the same thing with sanctification, or as something consequent upon it. I believe justification to be wholly distinct from sanctification, and necessarily antecedent to it.

Works XIX, 96.

From the moment we are justified, there may be a gradual sanctification, a growing in grace, a daily advance in the knowledge and love of God.

Jackson VIII, 329.

When we are born again, then our sanctification, our inward and outward holiness begins. And thenceforward we are gradually to "grow up in him who is our head."

Works II, 198.

Salvation is carried on by "convincing grace," usually in Scripture termed "repentance" which brings a larger measure of self-knowledge, and a farther deliverance from the heart of stone. Afterwards we experience the proper Christian salvation; whereby, "through grace" we "are saved by faith," consisting of those two grand branches, justification and sanctification. By justification we are saved from the guilt of sin, and restored to the favour of God; by sanctification we are saved from the power and root of sin, and restored to the image of God.

Works III, 204.

Entire sanctification, or Christian perfection, is neither more nor less than pure love—love expelling sin and governing both the heart and life of a child of God. The Refiner's fire purges out all that is contrary to love, and that many times by a pleasing smart.

Jackson XII, 432.

Certainly till persons experience something of the second awakening, till they are feelingly convinced of inbred sin so as earnestly to groan for deliverance from it, we need not speak to them of present sanctification. We should first labour to work that conviction in them. When they feel it and hunger and thirst after full salvation, then is the time to show them it is nigh at hand, it may be received just now by simple faith.

Letters, VI, 144–45.

A will steadily and uniformly devoted to God is essential to a state of sanctification, but not an uniformity of joy or peace or happy communion with God. These may rise and fall in various degrees; nay, and may be affected either by the body or by diabolical agency, in a manner which all our wisdom can neither understand nor prevent.

Jackson XII, 398.

Indeed, this I always observe wherever a work of sanctification breaks out the whole work of God prospers. Some are convinced of sin, others justified, and all stirred up to greater earnestness for salvation.

Journal VI, 73.

Therefore they [the Methodists] maintain with equal zeal and diligence the doctrine of free, full, present justification on the one hand, and of entire sanctification both of heart and life on the other being as tenacious of inward holiness as any mystic, and of outward as any Pharisee.

Works III, 507.

If you seek it [sanctification] by faith, you may expect it as you are: and if as you are, then expect it now. It is of importance to observe that there is an inseparable

connection between these three points: expect it by faith,
expect it as you are, and expect it now! To deny one of
them is to deny them all: to allow one is to allow them all.
Works II, 169.

I believe it [sanctification] to be an inward thing, namely,
the life of God in the soul of man; a participation of the
divine nature; the mind that was in Christ; or, the renewal
of our heart after the image of Him that created us.
Journal, II, 275.

A gradual growth in grace precedes [sanctification], but
the gift itself is always given instantaneously. I never knew
or heard of any exception; and I believe there never
was one.
Letters, III, 213.

Gradual sanctification may increase from the time
you was justified; but full deliverance from sin, I believe,
is always instantaneous. At least, I never yet knew an
exception.
Letters, VIII, 190.

Scripture

All Scripture is inspired of God—The Spirit of God not
only once inspired those who wrote it, but continually
inspires, supernaturally assists, those that read it with ear-
nest prayer.
Explanatory Notes: 2 Tim. 3:16.

I therein build on no authority, ancient or modern, but
the Scripture. If this supports any doctrine, it will stand;
if not, the sooner it falls the better. Neither the doctrine

in question [Christian Perfection] nor any other is anything to me, unless it be the doctrine of Christ and His Apostles.

Jackson XI, 449.

On Scripture and common sense I build all my principles. Just so far as it agrees with these I regard human authority.

Jackson XII, 476.

It is easily discerned that these two little words, I mean faith and salvation, include the substance of all the Bible, the marrow, as it were, of the whole Scripture.

Works II, 156.

The Scriptures are the touchstone whereby Christians examine all, real or supposed, revelations. In all cases they appeal "to the law and to the testimony," and try every spirit thereby.

Jackson X, 178.

The Holy Scripture containeth all things necessary to salvation; so that whatsoever is not read therein, nor may be proved thereby, is not to be required of any man that it should be believed as an article of faith, or be thought requisite or necessary to salvation.

Article of Religion V, Book of Discipline, 58.

[S]cripture interprets scripture; one part fixing the sense of another. So that, whether it be true or not, that every good textuary is a good Divine, it is certain none can be a good Divine who is not a good textuary.

Jackson X, 482.

God in Scripture commands me, according to my power, to instruct the ignorant, reform the wicked, confirm the virtuous.

Works XXV, 615.

Sin

So that no man sins because he has not grace, but because he does not use the grace which he hath.

Works III, 207.

As a very little dust will disorder a clock, and the least sand will obscure our sight, so the least grain of sin which is upon the heart will hinder its right motion toward God.

Jackson XI, 438.

I spent two or three hours in the House of Lords. I had frequently heard that this was the most venerable assembly in England. But how was I disappointed? What is a lord but a sinner, born to die!

Journal, VII, 46.

Two old members recovered I make more account of than three new ones. I love to see backsliders return.

Jackson XII, 452.

Nay, remember, there can be no little sin, till we can find a little God!

Works III, 383.

Even he who now standeth fast in the grace of God, in the faith that "overcometh the world," may nevertheless fall into inward sin, and thereby "make shipwreck of his faith."

Works I, 443.

[A]ll sin is of an infectious nature.

Works IX, 260.

Be ashamed of nothing but sin: Not of fetching wood
(if time permit) or drawing water; not of cleaning your
own shoes, or your neighbour's.

Jackson VIII, 310.

An unawakened child of the devil sins willingly; one that
is awakened sins unwillingly; a child of God "sinneth not,
but keepeth himself, and the wicked one toucheth him
not."

Works I, 263.

Know your disease! Know your cure! Ye were born in sin;
therefore "ye must be born again," "born of God."

Works II, 185.

Who can number the sands of the sea, or the drops
of rain, or thy iniquities?

Works I, 227.

Let us therefore hold fast the sound doctrine "once delivered to the saints," and delivered down by them with the
written word to all succeeding generations: that although
we are renewed, cleansed, purified, sanctified, the moment
we truly believe in Christ, yet we are not then renewed,
cleansed, purified altogether but the flesh, the evil nature,
still remains (though subdued) and wars against the Spirit.
So much the more let us use all diligence in "fighting the
good fight of faith." So much the more earnestly let us
"watch and pray" against the enemy within.

Works I, 333–34.

We are not to fight against notions but sins.

Works XXVI, 268.

A denial of original sin not only renders baptism needless with regard to infants, but represents a great part of mankind as having no need of Christ, or the grace of the new covenant. I now speak of infants in particular, who, if not "guilty before God," no more need the merits and grace of the Second Adam than the brutes themselves.

Jackson IX, 429.

But though we readily acknowledge, "he that believeth is born of God," and "he that is born of God does not commit sin," yet we cannot allow that he does not feel it within: it does not reign, but it does remain.

Works I, 336–37.

That vice is the parent of misery, few deny.

Works III, 568.

Ease bought by sin is a dear purchase.

Works II, 257.

Nothing is sin, strictly speaking, but a voluntary transgression of a known law of God. Therefore every voluntary breach of the law of love is sin; and nothing else, if we speak properly.

Jackson, XII, 394.

The thing is plain. All in the body are liable to mistakes, practical as well as speculative. Shall we call them sins or no? I answer again and again, Call them just what you please.

Jackson, XII, 239.

I believe there no such perfection in this life as excludes these involuntary transgressions which I apprehend to be naturally consequent on the ignorance and mistakes inseparable from mortality. . . . Therefore Sinless perfection is a phrase I never use, lest I should seem to contradict myself.

Jackson XI, 396.

One just saved from sin is like a newborn child, and needs as careful nursing.

Jackson XII, 273.

Singing

[The Methodists sing] not lolling at ease, or in the indecent posture of sitting, drawling out one word after another, but all standing before God and praising Him lustily and with good courage.

Jackson XIII, 217.

Is not this formality creeping in already, by those complex tunes, which it is scarcely possible to sing with devotion? Such is, "Praise the Lord, ye blessed ones." Such the long quavering hallelujah annexed to the morning-song tune, which I defy any man living to sing devoutly.

Jackson VIII, 318.

Sing lustily and with a good courage. Beware of singing as if you were half dead, or half asleep; but lift up your voice with strength.

United Methodist Hymnal, vii.

Social Religion

I shall endeavor to show that Christianity is essentially a social religion, and that to turn it into a solitary religion is indeed to destroy it.

Jackson V, 296.

Whatever religion can be concealed is not Christianity.
Works I, 540.

"Holy solitaries" is a phrase no more consistent with the
gospel than holy adulterers. The gospel of Christ knows
of no religion, but social; no holiness but social holiness.
Jackson XIV, 321.

Stewardship

Gain all you can without either hurting yourself or your
neighbor, in soul or body, by applying hereto with unin-
termitted diligence, and with all the understanding which
God has given you. Save all you can, by cutting off every
expense which serves only to indulge foolish desire, to
gratify either the desire of the flesh, the desire of the eye,
or the pride of life. Waste nothing, living or dying, on
sin or folly, whether for yourself or your children. And
then, give all you can, or in other words give all you have
to God.
Works II, 278–79.

Much money does not imply much sense; neither does a
good estate infer a good understanding. As a gay coat may
cover a bad heart, so a fair peruke [wig] may adorn a
weak head.
Jackson IX, 230.

You do not consider, money never stays with me; it would
burn me if it did. I throw it out of my hands as soon as
possible, lest it should find a way, into my heart.
Letters, V, 108–9.

S

You do not know the state of the English Methodists. They do not roll in money, like many of the American Methodists.

Jackson XIII, 70.

Who can gain money without in some measure losing grace!

Jackson XIII, 33.

And hear ye this, all you who have discovered the treasures which I am to leave behind me: if I leave behind me ten pounds (above my debts and the little arrears of my fellowship) you and all mankind bear witness against me that "I lived and died a thief and a robber."

Jackson VIII, 40.

What is money to me? Dung and dross. I love it as I do the mire in the streets.

Letters. V, 13.

These money-lovers are the pest of every Christian society. They have been the main cause of destroying every revival of religion. They will destroy us, if we do not put them away.

John Wesley. Addenda to the Minutes of Some Conversations, 1781. Q32

Time

Meanwhile redeem the time, catch the golden moments as they fly.

Letters, VII, 241.

No idleness can consist with growth in grace. Nay, without exactness in redeeming time, you cannot retain the grace you received in justification.

Jackson VIII, 315–16.

And God's time is always the best time.

Works II, 148.

A little fatigue I do not regard, but I cannot afford to lose time.

Letters, VI, 208.

Be punctual. Do everything exactly at the time. And, in general, do not mend our Rules, but keep them; not for wrath, but for conscience sake.

Jackson VIII, 310.

Beware of foolish desire! Beware of inordinate affections! Beware of worldly cares! But, above all, I think you should beware of wasting time in what is called innocent trifling.

Jackson V, 68.

Tolerance

And yet nothing has done more disservice to religion, or more mischief to mankind, than a sort of zeal which has for several ages prevailed . . . pride, covetousness, ambition, revenge, have in all parts of the world slain their thousands, but zeal its ten thousands.

Works III, 309.

[F]ervour for opinions is not Christian zeal. But how few are sensible of this! And how innumerable are the mischiefs which even this species of false zeal has occasioned in the Christian world!

Works III, 317–18.

Trinity

How do the rays of the candle brought into the room instantly disperse into every corner? Again: here are three candles, yet there is but one light. Explain this, and I will explain the Three-One God.

Works II, 381.

After all the noise that has been made about mysteries, and the trouble we have given ourselves upon that head, nothing is more certain than that no child of man is required to believe any mystery at all. With regard to the Trinity, for instance, what am I required to believe? Not the manner wherein the mystery lies. This is not the object of my faith; but the plain matter of fact. "These Three are One." This I believe, and this only.

Jackson XIII, 30.

[T]he knowledge of the Three-One God is interwoven with all true Christian faith, with all vital religion.

Works II, 385.

Work/Diligence

And if ever I should listen to that siren song, "Spare thy life." I believe my Master would spare me no longer, but soon take me away.

Jackson XIII, 4.

God grant I may never live to be useless!

Journal, VI, 428.

I am called to work: you are called to suffer. And if both these paths lead to the same parish, it is enough.

Letters, VII, 317.

Leisure and I have taken leave of one another. I propose to be busy as long as I live, if my health is so long indulged to me. In health and sickness I hope I shall ever continue, with the same sincerity.

Jackson XII, 20.

[I]t is impossible that an idle man can be a good man, sloth being inconsistent with religion.

Works III, 269.

[Y]ou will frequently see little fruit of all your labour. But leave that with Him. The success is His. The work only is yours.

Jackson XIII, 23.

And without industry we are neither fit for this world nor for the world to come.

Works III, 392.

It is incumbent on all that are justified to be zealous of good works. And these are so necessary that if a man willingly neglect them, he cannot reasonably expect that he shall ever be sanctified.

Works II, 164.

Never be unemployed a moment. Never be triflingly employed. Never while away time.

Jackson VIII, 309.

To continual watchfulness and prayer ought to be added continual employment. For grace fills a vacuum as well as nature, and the devil fills whatever Gods does not fill.

Jackson XI, 439.

Wherever the work of our Lord is to be carried on, that is my place for today. And we live only for today; it is not our part to take thought for tomorrow.

Jackson XII, 496.

World

I look upon all the world as my parish; thus far I mean, than in whatever part of it I am, I judge it meet, right, and my bounden duty to declare, unto all that are willing to hear, the glad tidings of salvation. This is the work which I know God has called me to. And sure I am that His blessing attends it.

Works XXV, 616.

I have long since shook hands with the world.
(Susanna Wesley to John Wesley)
Journal, III, 33.

CPSIA information can be obtained
at www.ICGtesting.com
Printed in the USA
BVHW070219270720
584565BV00004B/26

9 781945 935787